Email Marketing

By Luigi Padovesi

Summary

Email Marketing 1

A Great Opportunity 5

What is a Newsletter 10

Set Goals...15

Transactional Emails 19

What is the Online Form 22

The Autoresponder 25

Spam: How to Ruin Yourself.....................29

Customer Trust 34

Call to Action 37

Our Strengths: SWOT Analysis 41

Increase visits 48
    Open rate 48
    Aim for the right target 55
    Copy strategy 59
    Inactive customers 63
    The advertising campaign 69
    The buying process 74

Mistakes to Avoid in Email Marketing 78

The Importance of Statistics 84

Lead Magnet: How to Attract Customers .. 88

New Techniques 100
    Lead Nurturing 100
    Webinar: Useful Information at your Fingertips 105
    The perfect trigger 109

The Importance of Feedback 112

Disclaimer..117

A Great Opportunity

Before talking about email marketing, we need to understand why it is better to focus on this tool and not using social media, for example.

The email or 'electronic-mail' was created with the intention of facilitating a conversation while maintaining an 'intimate' style. This is an imitation of when paper letters were exchanged through the mail or passed by hand. It gives a feeling of trust, security and confidence between the sender and the recipient.

It's also a much more professional tool than a social platform, since its sole purpose is to put two people in conversation through an online 'letter' system. The email is a tool with a great potential that we can still exploit. However, it is very important to understand when and how to use it; The possibility that our email will be opened in the first hour of being received is very high, while as time passes the chances of someone opening and taking an interest in our proposal falls dramatically.

Therefore, creating email marketing means creating campaigns and marketing strategies using email, without spam, as a main tool. Through this tool, we can take advantage of various methods to send our customers a clear and direct message. The most common method is the newsletter, which we will discuss later. Email marketing is considered to be the best method to retain customers. It has a very high percentage of return on investment (ROI) compared to other techniques because it is an easy, fast and direct tool when used to promote an offer, proposal, novelty, price list, etc. Furthermore, it also allows us to visualize how many people are interested in our offer when we see who has opened the email. We can practically monitor our strategy in real time.

When described, it seems like a medium for everyone and it is!
However, there are several errors that many people make, which consequently has a negative impact on the ROI. One of these common errors is email spam. Just think: a person has voluntarily registered and is interested in our proposal, but after a few days they have 20 emails from us with all the various offers ... It is very intrusive, and

we are going to suffocate what should be our success. It is better to send even a single email that better describes who we are, what we do and what we offer.

What is a Newsletter

The newsletter is a very widespread tool in the marketing sector. Its main objective is to keep our customers updated. We can present new offers, products and promotions, among other things, to customers who have explicitly asked to stay updated on our business. This avoids excessive spam of intrusive and useless messages. The newsletter can be used not only to present news, but also to provide information, such as assistance for a product.

Therefore, it is a very advantageous tool for companies that want to keep their customers up to date on specific products or promotions, but it is also an advantage for professionals who are looking for advertising and new customers. Creating your own newsletter campaign does not require a high level of investment, since it is an inexpensive tool, but it requires a commitment to creating an email that attracts customers. To take full advantage of the newsletter it is best to write a short message with easy words that can be read within a short time. It should be easy to read for any type of customer and above all it invites people to take a better interest in our proposal, so that they can become potential customers in the future. At the beginning of this email we must say what we are proposing in an intriguing way. We must express the details of our event and what products or offers we want to propose. Of course, it is essential to use newsletters, but this does not mean we should underestimate all other means of email communication we can use to present ourselves to the market in the best possible way.

Have you ever thought of how many newsletters arrive to you every day? I'll give you a small example of someone accepting the conditions for us to send emails to them 'without them knowing'. They are looking for a free online ebook with the main topic "production". They come across a site where you can download the book at no cost. They click the download button ... But the file was not downloaded because they did not register with the site. So, there is a pop-up button to register. To register and download the book, they must provide an email and a password to to log in every time. They have provided their email, and over time they will find several emails from the free ebook download site. The sites or other sources we register with to obtain a product is where most of our emails come from.

Set Goals

The first thing that needs to be done before starting any economic activity is setting a clear, fixed goal. We must know what we want to gain, why we are doing this and if it is really worth investing time and money or if it is simply a waste of time. Then we may put in place all the plans we have thought of through the various resources available and the various investments. Since email marketing is a very complex tool, before realizing our plans we should understand how we want to use this system and what we want to achieve. For example, we have adopted a system to:

- Increase the number of customers who see what we want to offer every day
- Promote your brand through promotions and offers
- Make ourselves known to new people
- Increase sales

We must therefore set ourselves some goals of where we want to arrive, but with our feet on the ground, avoiding useless objectives to which we will never arrive. For objectives such as those I listed above we should try to establish a time frame in which we want to complete all these goals. This is so we can properly organize the structure of the activity, monitor the progress of our journey towards what we are aiming for and understand why we are doing what we are doing.

The goal of an activity is not always profit oriented, such as in associations, which may have a purpose in helping the community. However, in our case the main objective is to achieve a profit, we are profit oriented. This is making money through the sale of products or services. However, we are not always able to reach our goals. This can happen when the various costs are too high and are greater than revenues. What can be done in this case is to start over with a new, well-structured marketing plan and learn from the mistakes made in the past.

Transactional Emails

Transactional emails are emails that inform us of a determined action that we have accomplished or of what is missing for the compilation of a fact. Compared to commercial emails, this type has a higher open rate, since they are not intended to promote something new but simply to inform about a fact already chosen by the customer. The transactional emails are, for example, emails that notify us and confirm when we have changed the password of our account, when we have correctly registered to a site or when we have successfully placed an order and it has been sent. This type of email contains useful information for the customer and has the task of reminding the recipient that he is our client, updating him on the various facts and promotions we are proposing. We can insert a small timed promotion in this type of email, for example: "You have registered on our site! To thank you we have prepared for you a 30% discount voucher on the next purchase you make from us, valid until next week!" so as not to lose it.

Or they can simply be confirmation emails, for example when we register for an online service and are asked to verify the email address we entered by clicking the link in the email sent. In the first few lines of the email we need to describe the contents of the latter.

What is the Online Form

When a customer registers on our site, we can choose certain information that he must provide us in order to use our service. We can ask him for his email, his name and surname, his age, where he lives and what work he does. We then present him with a form to complete with all his personal information, this is an online form. This information can be very useful for getting to know the customer we are addressing and understanding what type of offer we can propose and when, so that our proposal be successful. For example: Maria is 35 years old and works in a shop where she is a hairdresser. To understand what kind of offer to make them first we need to know the age and profession, in this case 35 years and hairdresser. The question is ... what kind of product could we propose?

We could offer a product that could be useful for her work or for leisure time, such as an innovative latest-technology hair dryer at a price not too high, perhaps adding a promotion. We certainly have a much better chance of encouraging Maria to buy from us if we offer her something that can actually be useful for her work or leisure, instead of presenting her with a useless object that can serve no purpose, for example, a product that can be used by another person. Therefore, it is essential to ask questions to your client to understand what kind of product might be of interest to them and actually be useful to them.

The Autoresponder

When we talk about Autoresponders (automatic answer), we mean all messages (emails) that are sent in response automatically using an external software. This type of message serves to answer questions, needs and requests that are often made to us and to avoid handwriting the same thing to all the questions we are asked. We can set up a software that is tasked to automatically send a reply email with the message chosen by us for every need and every time a customer has a common question to ask us. Maybe in a day we find ourselves with 20 emails that have practically the same content, that have asked us the same question. Why answer each email individually and waste time when we can safely set a bot to do it, so that we can think about other problems and above all how to promote our business and find new customers. An example of an Autoresponder is when we register at a website and we must confirm our email via the electronic mailbox, or simply the welcome message that is sent to each individual user who has registered to a particular service. Think about having to welcome and explain your activity to every single person who registers in our service, it would be a mess. Autoresponder messages are chosen by us and used automatically. An example could be: "Welcome to our consulting service, we hope to be of help in all cases! If you need assistance, you can contact us at the email address below." or "The request for the creation of the account on our site has been sent ... Immediately confirm your email by clicking the button below". (etc.)

These messages can also be surveys or customer questions, to keep them the same each time. The only thing you should do is to change the name of the recipient each time.

Spam: How to Ruin Yourself

Spam is sending one or more messages, usually for advertising purposes, repeatedly on e-mail. From customers it is very annoying because it is very intrusive. Almost every day on our e-mail we receive at least two spam messages (advertising), which clogs the email inbox. Some of these emails are also unsafe, in fact many have a main objective to obtain information and steal personal data from people. Obviously when we talk about spam, we are not referring only to spam via email but also to on social networks and others. We can therefore establish that spam has, as its main objective, to reach many users and try to attract them to buy. But how do they find us? Simple, we are the ones who open the doors to these people. When? Just think of all the times we have left our email address in various sites to have a service offered by the site only by registration, or when we leave our phone number to win a contest. This is why it is important to take a look at the terms of certain sites. When we register to use a service they write "the email address provided, may be subject to a transfer to a third party". It's clear where all those emails or advertising calls come from. One way to avoid being subject to these advertisements is a temporary email that we can provide to the sites so that the advertisements are not addressed to our email, but to another email that will be self-destructed after a period of time that we use. This service can easily be found on certain sites that offer this benefit. Another useful function that is directly processed by the Gmail team is the anti-spam filter, which automatically deactivates and eliminates all those annoying advertising emails that we have not chosen to be sent to us. Spam aims to send a message to many unknown people who are certainly not in the least interested in the service or product. In chapter 2 we will understand better why it is important to aim for a suitable target and why sending your own promotional message to more people is to be avoided. In summary, to avoid ruining your online reputation and looking like a person who needs money and who doesn't know where and how to advertise their services or products, it's best to avoid unnecessary spamming to random and totally unknown people.

Customer Trust

Have you ever wondered if you really know your customers? Have you ever wondered if you're talking to the right people? If your visitors are really interested in your product or service? Some time ago it was very common to take a large number of unknown emails without exact origin and send them all a promotional message: practically a senseless choice and useless spam. (It would be better to send no more than 2 promotional emails per week). While we were the first to find our customers through spam, advertising and word of mouth, today it is no longer the case. In fact, it is the consumer who chooses from who to contact and who to buy for their needs. The advertisement issued by the seller serves only to give an idea, to promote a product that lists the utilities and the advantages and serves above all to show the public that we are better than the competition.

But this can only mentally influence the client's situation, in fact it is he who decides who to choose and through advertisements they get a better idea of what we offer. So, our success is determined above all by how we address customers, the reputation we have built over time and feedback from various buyers. Therefore, customers gain for themselves through the trusting relationship they have with us. To build a good reputation with customers, we must always be sincere and available on everything, such as being clear and sincere about all the purchase prices that are present before making any purchase.

Call to Action

The 'calls to action' are the action calls, that is all the buttons and links that have the purpose of calling the potential customer to one action, and then to complete a series of actions that we want. Such as those buttons where it says: "read on", "contact us" or "buy now".

Now I will list a series of tips to best set up your call to action and attract more people accordingly.

- Choose an appropriate contrast between the colors that differs from the rest of the site, or any other means of transmission. Setting colors that don't bother the eye and that are pleasant to look at is very important; in particular, avoid making two light colors close together since it reduces readability and increases visual discomfort.

- Try different types of call to action to understand which are liked by the customers, because if you like it, that doesn't mean visitors will like it too.
- Create a simple, direct and easy to identify call to action that attracts attention in a pleasant way
- Use a clear and pleasant font

- Make your call to action an unrepeatable opportunity, a timed offer that invites the potential customer to click on it.
- Write the advantages of registering for the advertising campaign, such as: 'Register now and get 1-month free trial.'

It is important to choose a design that unites the call to action and the site or platform in general. For example: The predominant color of your software is green, and the platform is white. Your button could be green with the white sign written in the center of it to match the platform.

Our Strengths: SWOT Analysis

Not everyone always manages to achieve their goals, since marketing strategies are not always adequate for their business. For this reason, even if we have great potential and talent, we cannot exploit it because we do not have the means or customers to achieve our goals. To understand why this is happening, we need to do a self-analysis, which means we must look at ourselves with the eyes of visitors and customers. It seems to us that everything is fine, that our products or services are actually useful to the customer, or that the way and the means by which we address the customer is perfect. However, in reality it is not, and this is confirmed to us by the number of sales and earnings registered each month.

The SWOT analysis determines the abilities, strengths and weaknesses of our economic activity and we have competition, and therefore also the strengths of those around us. The strengths of an activity or a small business are special features that make a positive difference from the competition; therefore, they are advantages that we can use against the competition. They can be for example:

- Certain skills or talents we possess to make a product or service in a better way than others
- A good reputation at the product or brand level
- If we have made special collaborations or for example worked abroad, I can say that "I worked abroad", which is a great goal that improves reputation above all. This means that we have great success and have contacted companies or people who need us in other countries, and means that we have a good knowledge of the language and the sector as we are working and relating to

people who are not aware of the language we speak mainly.

Once we have understood how to find our strengths and know what they are, we have also found an activity that succeeds better than the others, which we know how to do effectively. We can make the most of this factor to dedicate ourselves further to other activities that could be useful in the future, or even to have an extra competence that we can expose to the public.

The weaknesses, on which we must work to try to fix them all, are those factors that do not benefit us, that in the eyes of the customers appear shoddy and not very effective. It is very important to identify our weaknesses because they could become instruments of advantage for the competition. For example: A customer needs to contact us for any information before making a purchase, but our chat and conversation system to contact the customer is poor and not effective. The customer then decides to abandon us and to go to the competition that may have noticed this weakness of ours and exploited it to the fullest, creating a better method of conversation, such as a live chat through the assistance and the customer.

This situation can also be used as a great advantage though! In fact, we can use the method that we have just shown you in our favor. For example: One of our competitors presents an online service that is very complex to use.

There! we can work on the simplicity of the service to ensure that a customer prefers us even for this simple factor. The SWOT analysis therefore serves to determine the strengths and weaknesses of any economic entity.

Increase visits

Open rate

Before understanding how to increase the rate of visits, we must first understand what it is, then the open rate or open rate. When we talk about open rates, we mean that percentage of people who have clicked and opened your advertising launch through certain emails that are addressed to specific people. It is therefore the relationship between emails sent and those that have actually been opened and consequently read. To monitor the open rate, it is absolutely not a problem, since sending an email addressed to a certain public, you will be presented with a delivery code, which will indicate whether our email has been opened or simply ignored; and even if this email were opened, for example, 5 times, the counting does not progress and only one and single opening is registered. Obviously we will never have an opening rate of 100%, (this would mean that if we sent 60 people each an email, all 60 have opened it, taking into consideration the content), it is practically impossible, even a 60% percentage of open rate is by no means a foregone conclusion, just think that if we sent our email to 60 people, 36 of them opened it taking into consideration the content; if we think about it a bit, it is not a number to underestimate even if we always try to aim higher than what is reported in the latest statistics, (just think that large companies usually have an open rate of 30/40%).

Obviously the higher the percentage of open rates, the greater the number of people who are interested in our proposal and consequently we will have more chances to find possible really interested customers, with a positive feedback on our activity and above all on our earnings.

Getting good results and therefore a high rate of openings is not as easy and predictable as it seems, because the key to finding an effective method is to experiment continuously with new messages, new offers and new proposals, until we find one that will bring us many people who will open our message, and consequently a large number of people potentially interested in our service. A very important thing that you should always do when we want to send an email, is to understand first of all who we want to address (as we will explain you better later, it is useless to propose bags, for example, to a completely disinterested public), and as a second step, mention the name of the recipient in any message, even if it is a company or a natural person. To mention at the beginning the name of the person to whom we are addressing, for example, is a fact that makes the customer feel important, that we took some time to write an email specifically to him; doing this we avoid making our message look like the usual spam of offers, promotions or other invasive things, it must instead be a message well structured and consciously aimed at the right person. Another determining factor is what we set at the beginning of the message, which will be what the recipient will first see as a notification, which will make him decide whether to simply click delete email or go into our campaign. It is practically a key factor to "conquer" a potential customer, to do this we must try to propose a simple, innovative and direct message in a few lines of text; just think of the usual whining message that we will never open, such as:

"With us 20% discount on everything for the first month", we must try to express a concept in a "fun" way to make it attract and entice people to understand better what we are talking about, we must try to propose, not only a good offer, but also a different concept than usual. Finally it is important to choose a good timing, to understand what is the opportune moment to send a certain message to our recipient, many say that the most opportune moment to enter the scene is at the center of the day, at the center of the week. But surely sending a message at 11.00 pm, or at 6.00

am, is not really such a strategic move to use.

Aim for the right target

We have thought of everything to start a successful business, we have created a simple, fast and effective website, a good method to let us know, an effective method to provide assistance and a good service. The problem is, however, that customers continue to leave without even spending a penny, even if they prove interested (intrigued) by our offer and by what we offer. The problem where is it because we have done everything perfectly? Simple, we totally missed the target customers to advertise us. Target means target, that is to say of certain people to whom we should aim that we have the certainty that they are actually interested in our service or product; we therefore have a great chance that these visitors can be transformed into real customers. When we talk about target groups we refer instead to a group of more people with the same Interests, who have similar lifestyles or needs; we should always aim for a target group and propose and promote our advertising or our promotional message where all the advantages are listed, who we are and what we do. In order to understand who our target or target is, we need to know the visitor or client to whom we are referring, to understand what their needs and preferences are.

Everything we write in our public site or on any other tool that has the purpose of interfacing between us and the consumer, must therefore be entirely written specifically for the customer. The criteria to define one's own target are: sex, age, educational qualification, profession. This is to understand what we should propose: just think, how useless it would be to propose to a man an offer for a women's cosmetics store. We must also understand where we can promote our advertising campaign. As in the target, this too must be displayed on certain sites and not by chance; going back to the example above, surely a cosmetics shop would be better to advertise it on a site that targets women. Just think about how useless it would be to advertise a cosmetics store on a gym site, for example. The most successful advertisements are those made directly by the browser, which can be found easily around, without having to look for them at certain sites.

Copy strategy

The copy strategy is practically a document that describes all the key strategies of any advertising campaign. It has the task of providing all the information useful to an activity to undertake the road to success, in this document they are mainly described:

- The advantages of purchasing our product. Why should a customer choose our service or product? What differentiates us from others? What advantages do we offer? (For example: resistance, lightness and simplicity)

- If we keep all the promises we have presented to our conquering customers. For example, a consumer bought our product and was disappointed with the quality of it because it is not as we described it before he made the purchase.
- How we present our product and service to the public. The presentation of a product is essential for a successful campaign, and to be able to do this, we must mainly use conversation. When we talk about conversation we don't want to give a false idea that it looks good or manipulate the customer's mind, but simply try to best

expose our product by saying all the strengths it has. Like a gift box, practically. The more beautiful it is externally, the more quality the content will be and consequently the greater the satisfaction of the owner.

- Availability. Are we always available to ship and sell products or provide a specific service? Are we always available to provide customer assistance?
- Brand trust. What reputation have we created over time? Are we a valuable brand or a poor quality one?

These are some of the fundamental criteria we need to think about before starting a business.

Inactive customers

Inactive customers are all those customers who have bought from us one or more times, but who have no longer made purchases for several weeks or months. Users who have registered inactive who have signed up for our campaign are practically useless and represent an expense of time. When a customer registers, we know practically everything about him, work, hobbies and necessity if we have obviously subjected him to some previous survey. Before understanding how to reactivate a client, we need to be clear about why he switched from active to inactive; we must understand our mistakes and where we could improve in the future. The main factors are:

- The customer is no longer interested in our offer even though we have best exposed our theses and received a clear and direct message.
- The customer does not receive our messages as he never uses his e-mail box.
- The customer is not convinced of our proposal. This happens when we have not

dealt well with the public and we have not transmitted our message.

- The customer is satisfied. That is when the customer no longer needs our service because he needed this only in a certain period of the past, but now he no longer needs anything from us as we have satisfied his need. When he joined, he needed something that we successfully provided and solved the case.

To identify those people who are no longer active or who have simply stopped caring about us, we need to check who among all the newsletters we sent, discarded them or never opened them. Now we could do to make users who have stopped caring about us active again. We must start from the assumption that a user who has already registered in the past, has already given us his confidence in us, and it is therefore easier to return an inactive customer, as he was in the past, than to conquer a new customer. But if our old client didn't respond even after we insisted with more than 5 newsletters, it means it's time to change group targets and ignore the past.

The main things to understand to try to reactivate customers are:

- Identify which customers have become inactive and understand why this happened.
- Try to catch the customers' attention.
- Make a proposal so revolutionary that it will immediately bring customers back.
- Wait and let it go.

These are just some of the many things you should do to try to get an inactive user back. However, if you send too many emails to people who have decided to ignore you, you only ruin your reputation; you should instead think about how to make new customers. The rate of inactive users also determines whether an advertising campaign is effectively effective, or not. In fact, the lower the percentage of inactive users, the greater our success, as most of our customers have clearly received our message.

The advertising campaign

The advertising campaign is the means by which any economic activity is exposed to the public to show the product or service that it wants to sell, to describe its quality, price and efficiency. The advertising campaign is fundamental when we talk about marketing, since it is practically considered the envelope of something, like the packaging of a gift; more beautiful is presented externally and the more chance we have of someone buying it. Before creating your own advertising campaign we must take into account the badget that we have available and we must decide to whom we want to focus and what are the objectives of our advertising campaign. To present an effective message that positively affects the customer we must:

- Express the benefits that the purchase of it will offer.
- Describe its usefulness.
- Send the price into the background, as a factor of second importance.

The advertising campaign can be one, which is repeated over time, or there may be more advertising different from each other but which have the same bases and the same intentions. Once a good advertising campaign has been established, we need to understand whether it is actually useful or not; to do this we have to go and see how many daily clicks we record.

Nowadays, however, it is quite complex to make a successful advertisement, since the client sees them all as something tiring and repetitive. Creativity and imagination are therefore fundamental factors for the creation of an effective advertising campaign since each campaign, behind the screen, has a complex history behind it. We therefore need to find and interpret our ideas in the best possible way, so that they are best understood by all consumers.

We have to decide several factors including language, for example. We can choose whether to make a serious and very professional advertisement, or whether to play a bit on the various themes to have a more confident and familiar bond with the customers. The visual language is also important, choosing a certain situation rather than another based on the context we want to propose is essential for a successful campaign. Obviously graphics, design and advertising in general must be relevant and above all consistent with what we really want to offer on the market or the service we offer.

The buying process

The buying process is practically the process that the consumer performs before getting to buy a certain product or service. This process lists all the strategies used to encourage the consumer to buy. This process is divided into several parts, including:

- Customer needs. At this stage we must interpret the customer's needs, to understand what kind of service or product we can offer. We must therefore look for the problem that the consumer intends to solve through our help. For example, our customer needs a new car, so we can offer a new car at a favorable price.

- The proposal at the right time. After the consumer has found a need, he is looking for a bargain at a low price and with immediate availability. And this is where we come into play, through an advertisement, we must propose an unmissable proposal. However, we must adapt to the economic situation of each individual customer, since before making the purchase, the customer always checks all the offers that have been proposed to him and consequently will choose the most advantageous one that best meets his needs, where he will have to spend less. .

- Customer decision. This is the penultimate step, or the one where the customer chooses what and from whom to buy.
- As the last step in the purchasing process we have the review. After the customer has made the purchase he will decide to write a review (feedback), based on how satisfied he is, whether we have interpreted and handled his problem as well as possible, or if he has been disappointed because we

have not kept our promises. However, this results in a huge decrease in purification level.

In other words, the phases are: Need, Knowledge, Evaluation, Purchase, Review.

Mistakes to Avoid in Email Marketing

- Many times, when we use email to satisfy, promote an advertisement or to talk with a client, we often make several mistakes that could send us on the wrong path. The most common mistakes made by those who want to take the path of email marketing are

- Send too many emails on the same day to the same consumers. This concept applies both when we want to send more emails in the same week, as when we send a newsletter to our customers every day. All this becomes very invasive for the one who receives our emails, making it him upset and he blocks all the emails we want to send him.

- Propose the same concept several times. This happens when we sent an email to a client and it was successful, proposing and describing our ideas or product. After we have noticed that our email was successful, we then decide to send the same email again, or by changing some terms to the same customer. It is a mistake to be avoided in order not to tire the customer and make him run away.

- Write to avoid appearing inactive. This happens when after sending a message that has been successful, we no longer know what kind of concept to propose or what message to send. Therefore, we decide to send superficial things and concepts that are useless. These useless messages will be immediately rejected by the recipients without even reading them.

- Improvise the contents of an email. When we write an email for a target, we need to know who we are targeting to understand what type of words to use and how to structure the email for each individual. Improvising at the last moment is absolutely wrong because to write an email we must first set up points to write in the email, such as: "promote a product, or provide information about what we do".

- Be in a hurry to send a message. As just mentioned, it would be advisable to write a list to be able to best send a message for the client. There is no hurry to send a message to the customer, since we have neither a deadline, nor the risk that if we do not send any email for a period of at least 7 days we will lose the customer. In short, take your time to set up a message that will work and hit where and how you want. To do this we can also use images attached, although it would be better to set your message more verbatim than by photo. The text must be useful, simple and must explain everything in the best way. A non-formal text style must be used, so we avoid using the third person as a form of courtesy. While the images must be captivating and simple, avoiding inserting too many concepts in a small space or inserting only text as nobody will read it.

The Importance of Statistics

Statistics are data collected over a specific period and route. Statistics have the task of making a person understand the various events that occurred during a predetermined period, topics such as: earnings, revenues, objectives achieved, strengths and weaknesses. A detailed analysis to draw up a list of all the statistics of your activity is usually made every weekend, at the end of the month or every year. The statistics therefore serve to determine the general situation and what has been done for a given period and aim to improve that figure for the future and how to do it. For example, this month we spent €200,000 for various overall expenses, and we made 30 sales of € 60.00 each, with a total revenue of € 1800.00, making the difference between the revenues and the total expenses, we therefore found a gain of € 1600.00.

Next month we are aiming to make a revenue higher than the previous month to increase the sum of earnings. To do this we must either increase the sales of a product or increase the price of it. The analysis of any economic activity is expressed through graphs or tables where all the data and phenomena that occurred during a certain period are inserted and described. This analysis is fundamental to establish new objectives and to understand the mistakes we have made. Taking time and doing a detailed analysis of the statistics means not only understanding how things are proceeding and if we are reaching our goals, but also making a self-assessment. To do this we can use certain software where all sales are described, the transactions and purchases we made every day. These software systems are also able to show general activity through percentages or direct numbers, relating earnings, revenues, expenses and any losses.

We can also use this tool to identify how things are progressing individually, so for each employee in part we can monitor the work done, the time taken or the sales made; so if something doesn't work in our business we don't blame our whole team, but we can go and analyze who actually is doing their job incorrectly.

Lead Magnet: How to Attract Customers

A Lead magnet is content designed specifically for the customer. It has the task of attracting the attention of consumers and above all convincing them and encouraging them to leave their contact information, such as their email address, so that we can interact with him over time. This factor is essential when we talk about marketing, as it is the basis of 'conquering' the customer before doing anything else. There are various strategies that we can use in a Lead magnet, they can be simple or complex and the most important thing is time, and above all, knowing how to wait. To give an example of a lead magnet we propose this situation: A consumer is looking for a course on how to improve the open rate, he comes across a site where he can download the appropriate file. He must first provide his email. In this case the lead magnet is the service in exchange for the email to which we could send various offers or discounts in the future. It is therefore a content:

• Completely free of charge for those who need it

- Easily obtainable by exchanging contact information, such as e-mail
- Can be downloaded by everyone at any time

The main objective is to help us set up a list with all contacts and potential customers by choosing an appropriate target. Then in the future we could send emails to entice the purchase of the good or service we are offering. It is also useful for showing your professional image to a wide audience of people who will make a good impression of us, positively increasing our reputation, and we enter the mind of those who buy. This means that every time you think of a product that we offer, you will think of us. Customers usually buy only from those who they trust and actually know or have already had purchased from in the past. Furthermore, this system is able to attract a large number of people, including people who are interested in buying. We then have a target to which we aim, then from there narrow to only consumers who actually intend to buy from us. The larger the number of people we are able to give us their email address, the more possibilities there are to find more potential customers and increase profits.

The Lead Magnet therefore represents the first step on the road towards the purchase. It must be structured properly to give the impression of a serious and professional proposal. It must include content that can establish a first relationship of trust between you and the customer. They must make a transition from "I'm looking for someone to help me" to "I found the perfect person for me" only through this first step. Our main objective is that when they intend to buy, they prefer to buy with us, thinking of the competition as an alternative, uncomfortable and ineffective way. As mentioned above there are various types of free Lead Magnets that we can establish, including:

● If we offer a service or a free trial for a certain period that expires with the purchase proposal
● Discounts or with offers on the final purchase
● A video file that best describes the service or product we offer in a simple and direct way. This type of video must be short and

appealing, with a nice design and must aim to show us as a trusted seller

In short, we can count on a high number of solutions. Obviously, we will choose the most appropriate and relevant one based on the service we offer.
We could do a self-assessment, thinking ... If I were in the customer's shoes, would I give my email in exchange for this service? Is it really worth it?

Now let's see how to create a Lead Magnet and what fundamental characteristics it must have to be effective and downloaded, presenting quality content. The first step in understanding how to create a quality lead magnet that is useful is to know who we are addressing and the problem or need for our product or service. For example, we know that we are turning to an online product seller, we could offer some sort of guidance on how to increase sales and customers. It is practically the same concept used by stores to attract customers. Just think: winter has begun, a clothing store has put on sale all winter clothes like jackets or sweatshirts. Surely the number of customers will increase after this strategic sale. The only difference between an online activity and the clothing store is that in the online activity the proposals are made based on the customer's knowledge, instead in the shop based on other factors. We don't know who our customers are as we turn to a vast number of people who can buy from us and not to individual targets.

In our case knowing how to help the customer is fundamental. Among all the customer's needs we must try to satisfy the most urgent one so that he will come back to us also in the future. Before exposing a solution to a certain customer product that we found we must be clear on how we want to solve the problem. Explain step by step how to solve the problem, using terminology that is not too complex. Be direct and avoid presenting a hasty and inadequate response, take your time, reflect and be informed so that you can set up a message of success that attracts the customer. Focus on one problem and satisfy it well, remember that this is only the first step towards the customer, so you have to give a sample of your skills and of what you know how to do! The customer must quickly understand the mistakes he has made or the information he needs. If he cannot understand what you are saying as it is too long a message with complex terminology and poor design, he will surely ignore and forget about us. Since the Lead Magnet is free, we must avoid uploading and divulging too much information that could possibly be useful in the future for solving a problem.

The lead magnet, therefore, is not only a tool to attract as many customers as possible, but it is a means that should not be underestimated as it is the first step to have the customer's trust. We must express ourselves and make ourselves understood perfectly. Our only purpose is to give our customer a contact so that in the future when we send a proposal or an advertising campaign, he knows that he can trust us and that the advertising we have proposed presents a quality product or service.

New Techniques

Lead Nurturing

Lead nurturing is a marketing strategy with a main objective is to aim and ensure that we establish a conversation with the customer. This strategy does not serve to promote a product or a service such as in an advertising campaign, but is to establish and improve a direct relationship of trust and knowledge between the customer and the seller. This trust is used to have the customer to buy from the seller not only for the quality product or service he offers, but also for the relationship established between the two subjects. Doing this will also make the customer believe that the competition is an uncomfortable and unknown variant from which you should be wary. We must forget everything else and put the customer at the center of everything so we must listen to him and transmit as much trust as possible.

When we establish a direct conversation with the potential client we must communicate without being intrusive. We must be courteous and be seen as the one who can easily and simply solve all the problems that are proposed to us in a short time. We must convey credibility and trust, giving the impression of a true professional. First, we must show to the customer all things we are competent in and have knowledge of in order to aid them better, such as marketing consultancy or online sales. The consumer understands that a seller to be trusted when he not only thinks about earning and being advertised, but also thinks about his customers and the trust and esteem between the two.

But what tools are best for communicating with a potential customer?

- Social networks - Social media can be a useful tool to promote an advertising campaign but also to communicate with customers and provide useful information. Through this means we can more easily establish a relationship of trust
- Newsletters - Newsletters like social media are not just about promoting something, but we can use newsletters to talk directly with the customer, writing a welcome message and describing the product for example

Through the lead nurturing, the customer will see us through different eyes. He will see us as a professional who cares about his customers. This tool is essential to accompany the customer towards the purchase, since we can easily provide all the information he needs or quell any doubts in a short time. Obviously, the lead nurturing is not only addressed to new customers, but also to those that have already purchased from us, to ensure that they are not lost and forgotten. Since these people have already trusted our brand at least once, it would not make sense to abandon them when we can preserve them and have more chances that they will purchase from us in the future.

Webinar: Useful Information at your Fingertips

The word "webinar" comes from the fusion of terms web and seminar. The webinar is practically a lesson or a real online course that you can safely follow online from any device that has internet access. A webinar is often accessed by registering for a specific online course that can be free or paid. A webinar is a live lesson where you discuss directly with the customer as if in school. Through a specific live chat, the client can converse freely with the one who is supporting the lesson, asking questions or clarifications using typing or directly through their voice. A presentation or lesson lasts about 1 or 2 hours. To access these live lessons we must be registered at a specific site or forum in the case of a free webinar. Obviously there are many webinars where you can participate and learn a lot of new things, but not all of them are well structured and easy to understand, and certainly paid lessons will be structured and explained better than free ones. But we must also keep in mind who is directing the webinar. Just think that quality always wins over quantity, since a concept that maybe explained in a course in 2 hours can easily be explained better in 30 minutes. Everything depends on who we decide to buy from.

Avoid paying unnecessarily and wasting your time to access random webinars. Before buying, see if that person from whom you want to buy it has good reviews, how much they know and if they are competent in the field. Based on strengths and weaknesses you could choose courses that will help you improve in these points, thus having even if you have to spend a little, you still have a good teaching from which to understand the mistakes to avoid in the future.

If you need to buy one or more lessons online, the suggestions we offer are:

- Take notes. Surely you will not remember all the important things that have been reported to you, in fact it is essential to take notes or write down the most important things
- Request all the materials used during the live as they are an important source of knowledge and strategies. Materials such as videos, images, illustrations, statistics, etc.

The perfect trigger

Triggering means when a given action is completed, another one immediately starts countering. Trigger marketing consists in the sending of a determined message in a particular period of the year or when there is a determined period, time, an event etc. These messages arrive instantly, but only at the time set by the seller. Just imagine a trigger of a gun which is activated by itself, and therefore automatically, when a target is in view. Trigger marketing works just like that. In a given period, the message we preset is sent to certain people we have carefully selected. These messages must contain promotions for special occasions, such as: It's Valentine's Day. We have prepared 1 month before for this event, we have already talked and bought a box of chocolates from the supplier, and the only thing we have left to do is resell it all. So, we prepared our unmissable offer, the box of chocolates that usually costs € 5.00, we are selling it for € 2.50, a real bargain! The autoresponder sends the promotional message describing the product and the reduced price to our directed audience. The choice lies with the customer, whether to buy or not. This explains why when there is a day of celebration, a certain product is always offered to us by email.

The Importance of Feedback

Before understanding what feedback is, why it is needed and why it is useful, we must be clear that feedback does not serve to criticize negatively or worse, to insult a person, a product or a service. Feedback should be used to freely express one's opinion regarding a given product or service in a constructive and opportune way. Obviously I will not write under to a product that has not satisfied my requirements "it sucks", but I will have to insert a detailed and pertinent description to explain to both the seller and future buyers why we decided to leave a negative or positive review. We must then describe how we found ourselves using that particular product or service, if it actually solved our needs, its quality and if it is simple and practical to use among other things. Feedback or reviews are therefore all the information from those who have used our product or service which we receive and influence us positively or negatively. Feedback is not always the best, there is more possibility of receiving a negative review than a positive one as the one who must judge must do it sincerely, listing all the points against and points of weakness that he found in our proposal . The feedback serves to give us an idea of how we are placing ourselves on the market, to make us preform a self-assessment and understand what our strengths and weaknesses are, We can used this to understand where we can improve in order to succeed in increasing sales and quality of what we are proposing. Getting feedback from people outside our business also helps us to strengthen because of different points of view and knowledge. It would be best to get as much feedback as possible from more people to get a broad perspective on the product and allows us to focus more factors on which we should work. If you need to give feedback to a salesperson, never make a critique that you never want to receive. Don't be generic, instead explain why you decided to give ⅗ stars, for example. Never write only 2 words, but formulate a pertinent and appropriate body of text that best explains the reason for your choice. For example, we need to evaluate a wool hat and we decided to include a review of ⅗ stars, in the feedback we simply wrote "Good". It is not exactly the best. There is a difference between writing a simple "Good" and writing, for example, "Excellent material, keeping warm, just like in the description, the only problem I decided not to put 5 complete stars is because the print looks slightly ruined in a part." The feedback is not just for us to understand how our product is doing on the market, but also to other customers who are undecided whether to buy from us or not. Reviews are very important.

Disclaimer

All registered trademarks and logos mentioned in this book, including Amazon, belong to their respective owners.

The author of this book does not claim or declare any rights to these trademarks, which are mentioned only for educational and informational purposes.